The Inn on the Moor

A History of Jamaica Inn
by
Rose Mullins

Researched by Peter Mullins and Rose Marie Mullins

The Inn on the Moor,
A History of Jamaica Inn

PR Publishing (Cornwall),
1 Moorview,
Bolventor,
Launceston,
Cornwall PL15 7TS

A History of Jamaica Inn. The Inn on the Moor.
First Published 1998.

All rights reserved. No part of this publication may be reproduced, stored in a retrieval system or transmitted in any form whatsoever, without the prior written permission of the publisher. This book may not be lent, resold, hired out, or any way disposed of by way of trade in any form of binding or cover other than that in which it is published, and without a similar condition, including this condition being imposed on the subsequent purchaser.

A History of Jamaica Inn. The Inn on the Moor, is published by PR Publishing (Cornwall), a completely independent company. All copyrights acknowledged.

Printed by Ink Print, 3 Station Road, Okehampton, Devon.

Contents

Foreword		iii
Chapter one	Bodmin Moor	3
Chapter two	The Beginning of Jamaica Inn	16
Chapter three	Early Owners and Landlords	24
Chapter four	From Ghoulies and Ghosties	27
Chapter five	Bolventor	32
Chapter six	The War Years	42
Chapter seven	Fundamental Changes	61
Chapter eight	Alistair Maclean	70
Chapter nine	Significant Changes	73

Foreword

From my childhood I have been an avid reader of the books of Daphne Du Maurier, but until about twenty-five years ago the places she wrote about in Cornwall meant nothing to me. I was very fortunate in that when I first came to see Cornwall for myself, the weather was all it could be. The sun shone from dawn till dusk, the bluebells and campion smothered the hedgerows and everywhere I went I found entrancing and beautiful. This first impression was a lasting one. I fell in love with Cornwall there and then and it is a love affair that has lost none of its hold over the years. My family and I came regularly to Cornwall from then on, exploring more and more and discovering for ourselves all the places that we had read about. The one pilgrimage that we made on every visit was to the village of Bolventor and Jamaica Inn. I was drawn to it as a magnet and the subsequent changes to the old Inn over those twenty-five years have not - for me - lessened in any way that magnetism.

In early 1990 I was even more fortunate to be taken on by the owners of Jamaica Inn as a Curator for the Potter's Museum that is sited alongside the Inn, where I stayed until my retirement in 2003. I enjoyed my work and meeting people, doing my best to answer their questions, but it bothered me considerably that so little was known about the Inn and I often idly thought that I should do something about it - and consequently did nothing! In 1996 my brother-in-law came to work at the Inn, showing as much interest in his new surroundings as I had done and - with his help and encouragement - I began the task of trying to discover the history of this fascinating old Coaching Inn. Peter's help was invaluable and so, too, has been the help of many of the local people of Bolventor and the moors, people whose lives have been bound up with the village and Inn, as were the lives of their forefathers before them. These good folk talked to us at length and gave us valuable insight into a way of life now sadly gone. They willingly loaned us precious snapshots, old postcards and scrap books and were the main source of the information that constitutes the essence of this book, because it rapidly became clear to us that you could not separate the Inn from the village, or the village from the moor. They are all an integral part of each other and the history of Jamaica Inn is also the history of Bolventor and Bodmin Moor, for any building - however long standing and famous - is just a shell, a shell that needs human beings to bring it to life, to give it substance.

I heard many people who probably first visited the Inn a very long time ago, express regret and even anger about the alterations and extensions that have taken place there over the last thirty years, but they must realise that Jamaica Inn today is what it has always been from its beginnings - a business. It is a business which exists to cater to the needs of its customers, be they the weary intrepid travellers on foot or horseback, in the time before the Turnpike road, or the horsedrawn coach passengers and mail coaches, to the modern motorist and coach passenger today. Nowadays the Inn welcomes around half a million visitors to its doors every year. The extensions and modernisations have become as necessary now as the first extension built in the late 18th Century and long may Jamaica Inn continue to offer hospitality and shelter to tired wanderers and eager sightseers.

Rose Marie Mullins,
March 1998.

The first conversion of the stable to a bar in the 1950's.

CHAPTER ONE

Bodmin Moor

When dawn breaks upon the moor it is a daybreak like no other, for a Cornish moorland vista is all sky. The first glow of dawn touches the night sky, tinting any cloud with deep rose. The golden orb rises slowly, creating an arc of pale lemon and the midnight blue from the hours of darkness slowly turns to the faded wash of early morn and eventide. The craggy tors, with their western slopes deep in shadow, are shown in stark relief, but neither they nor the sweeping lower slopes, so green in the spring and summer, and clothed like the great plains in grasses the colour of ripe hay in autumn and winter, can detract from the awesome canopy above them with its ever changing scenes.

Such mornings break with liquid gold, the sunlight streaming low across the moor, casting long shadows. There is peace beyond measure, and beauty beyond price. The silence is broken only by skylark song and the sound of running water in rock-strewn, moorland streams, sparkling 'neath the sun. Their banks are covered with spikey tufts of reed and boggy mire, lichen covered granite boulders dotted all around. Cattle, sheep and moor ponies graze contentedly, buzzards soar and a lone curlew rests, and speaks with its whirring, clicking cry. Yellow furze and blackthorn flower everywhere atop the banks and hedgerows, which are in reality dry stone walls, erected by man over hundreds of years. In the Cornish fashion such walls are topped by sods of earth and are rapidly overgrown with vegetation, which turns them into havens for flora and fauna, including the all pervasive bracken which - however destructive - only enhances the scenery with its delicate feathery fronds of apple green and its autumnal splendour of russets and gold.

From the time of the first appearance of the snowdrop the moors are decked with flowers. The violets and primroses herald the first real sign of spring, which usually comes late to the moor. They are followed by bluebells, campion, wild orchid and cowslips and the deep fuschia pink of the foxglove trumpets its presence in great banks of colour before high summer when the flowers, so abundant, gradually die away. Little grows on the tors but sycamore. Oaks and lowland beeches flourish on the lower slopes and deep in the valleys. On the marshy ground heron, golden plover and dunlin alight, and among the gorse with its blazing golden blossom and honey scent, the linet, tit and willow warbler flit and perch and give forth song. The black and white dipper stands on a shallow rock in mid stream and 'dips' his plump little body in rhythm and the kingfisher swoops. Swallows and snipe abound and flocks of lapwing are often seen on Davidstow Moor. In May new born lambs frolic. They are born later because of their inhospitable surroundings and throughout the summer the newly born foals caper and prance on their ridiculously spindly legs, but seldom leave their mother's side. The ponies stand hock deep in the watering hole on Davidstow unless the summer is long and dry and then - when that waterhole dries up - they must look elsewhere, to Crowdy Reservoir or the moorland streams to slake their thirst. The days are long and the sunsets truly memorable, but these are the glory days and - though much more common than is generally supposed - it is not for such weather that the moors are justifiably famed.

Other dawns come that are barely discernible. The greyness lightens imperceptibly but the fog hangs like a great blanket, obscuring everything. Such mists can happen at any time of the year, and go as quickly as they come. Moisture hangs in the air like a damp shroud and clings to the hair and clothes, wetting almost as much as rain. The farm house and cottage lights are on all day, and even local people are wary of going far from all that is familiar, whilst the stranger to the moors should never venture off the roads for he would instantly be lost. It does not do to wander far off the beaten tracks, for there are treacherous bogs into which both man and beast have disappeared never to be seen again. The average rainfall for Cornwall is sixty-five to seventy inches a year. With its narrowing peninsular shape, thrusting out into the Atlantic, divided almost totally from Devon by the Tamar and practically surrounded by water, it is a land of tempest. The prevalent westerly gales crossing and building up over nearly 4,000 miles of ocean, sweep up across the land bending all before them, and the stunted, twisted blackthorn trees, biased against the wind, bear witness to their strength and fury. The gales can last for days and even fifteen miles inland from the sea, the salt spray still covers the earth and rots iron and wood and blackens plants and shrubs. Out at sea the big ships turn into the wind and drop anchor to ride out the storm, or make haste to reach port. The fishing fleets stay safely tied up in harbour. There is little shelter on the moor. The rain lashes down and is blown hither and thither, and finds its way through every crack and cranny. The wind howls and whines, doors and windows rattle, draughts come in everywhere to chill the bone. However extreme the weather it seems to affect the sheep and cattle not at all, but the ponies hate it. Belonging to the Moorland Farmers (Commoners), they stand huddled together, backs to the wind, in whatever bit of shelter they can find. Their heads are down, they neither move or graze, just stand there stoically enduring what they cannot alter. Little has changed on this black volcanic moorland since it was first populated some seven thousand years ago. Then, only the coastal fringes of Cornwall and the very

Moor Ponies at the watering hole on Davidstow.
Photograph by Rose Marie Mullins.

Mutual moorland cattle and canine curiosity.
Photograph by Rose Marie Mullins.

high ground of the moors were habitable, the rest was dense forest, almost impenetrable, where wild boar and deer abounded. The Neolithic (New Stone Age) men first cultivated with primitive ploughs, using only flint tools. They were followed by the Megalithic people from the South of France, and the Bronze Age men from Spain, known as the Beaker people because of their habit of burying small bronze beakers with their dead. The Bronze Age population on the moor was higher than it is today and they left behind the stone circles, megalith chamber tombs and hundreds of tumuli and barrows. Cornwall is singularly rich in archeological remains and prehistoric antiquities.

The Iron Age Celts came next, (approx. 200BC - 500AD) and they lived in hill fortresses or "rounds" and cliff castles, with very well constructed huts. They introduced the iron adzes and axes which enabled them to clear the undergrowth and dense forests, and they also brought in the wheeled plough. They were there when the Romans invaded, and lived in relative harmony with the invaders engaging in much trade since the Romans were only really interested in the ore trade, until they finally withdrew from Cornwall in 410AD. The Cornish tribes were known as the Dumnonii at the time of the invasion. It is thought that the mythical Arthur existed about this time, certainly before 600AD.

William the Conqueror presented the Earldom of Cornwall to his half brother, Robert of Mortain, and in 1337 The Black Prince was created the first Duke of Cornwall by his father, Edward III. From thence the male heir to the English throne is born the Duke of Cornwall. Much of the land on the moor is owned by the Duchy to this day.

The moors are dotted with ancient villages and hamlets, of which Bolventor is among the youngest. The traveller from the east comes first to Launceston as he crosses the River Tamar border and a few miles further on to the first of the villages that edge the moor, Five Lanes and Altarnun.

Altarnun is one of the most ancient villages in Cornwall. Deep in a valley, sheltered and quiet, it is also one of the prettiest. The name is a corruption of, 'the Altar of St. Nonna', (Ol-ter-Nun). St. Nonna was a Celtic missionary and mother of the Welsh St. David - after whom Davidstow is named. The present Church, known as The Cathedral of the Moors, was built in the 15th Century, but there is in the Churchyard a Celtic Cross dated AD 527, marking the end of St. Nonna's Pilgrimage, and there was a Nunnery on the site of the Church. It is also said that Altar Nun means, 'transfer from Nunnery to Parochial Church'. St. Nonna is reputedly buried there. It was the fictitious Vicar of Altarnun who figured largely in Daphne

Altarnun Bridge and Church.

Wesley Chapel at Trewint.

Du Maurier's book "Jamaica Inn".

The Parish records state that in Charles II's time, "In this Parish lived Peter Jowle, Deacon, who was 150 years old, and at the age of 100 new black hairs grew on his head, among the white, and new teeth grew to replace those long since lost."

Above Altarnun the village of Five Lanes has lost much of its former importance. The King's Head, one of the oldest Inns on the moor, was built around 1622, and until 1988 large cattle fairs were held here as they had been for hundreds of years.

To the west of Five Lanes lies the hamlet of Trewint. Here is the cottage built by Digory Isbell, who lived there with his wife, Elizabeth, in the eighteenth century. It was to this cottage that John Wesley and two of his followers, John Downes and John Nelson came, seeking shelter before they travelled further on into Cornwall to preach to the Cornish people about Methodism. The Isbells were among their first converts and Digory Isbell (a Stonemason by trade), added an extra room to his cottage to be used as a Chapel, in 1743. John Wesley made six visits to Trewint between 1744 and 1762 and the hamlet became the first stronghold in Cornwall of Methodism. To this day "Wesley Day" is still celebrated with an annual service at the cottage to commemorate its restoration. It was purchased by the North Hill Circuit in 1947 for the restoration, which was completed in 1950, and meetings are still held there.

Approaching Bolventor, to the left runs the road to St. Cleer. The ancient track and drover's route, which follows the River Fowey (pronounced Foy), crosses the river at Draynes Bridge - from the Cornish, Drenen, meaning Bridge of Thorns, which is probably the first bridge to cross the Fowey and was built around 1500. The farmers have the grazing rights to Draynes Common, the heath so named in 1362.

South of the A30 which crosses the moor, lie the villages of St. Neot, Warleggan and Temple, among others. Temple is one of the most ancient hamlets. Named after the Knight's Templar, warriors of the Crusades, it was founded in 1120AD as a Hospice for travellers, and continued until the middle of the 18th Century, when the Order of the Knight's Templar was dissolved. The Church was known for many years as the Gretna Green of Cornwall, where unscrupulous Clergy would marry anyone as long as they could pay for the privilege. Errant Vicars seem to be the order of the day on the moor, both fictional and real! The last resident Vicar of Warleggan fell out with his tiny congregation and locked them out of the Church. He shut himself up in the Vicarage and refused to speak to anyone, though he did hold Sunday

Scrubby moorland on Kerrow Downs.
Photograph by Rose Marie Mullins.

Summit of Roughtor

Services, preaching to a congregation of cardboard figures!

The highest village on the moor is St. Breward and the Church there dates from 1278. It was extensively restored in 1863, having been struck more than once by lightning.

Though not high by the standards of Dartmoor, still the tors on Bodmin Moor are impressive. As ancient as time itself they stand, their rocky outcrops weathered over millions of years to their present fantastic silhouettes, testament to the fact that there ARE some things that never change. The highest is Brown Willy at 1,375 ft. Its strange name is a corruption of the Cornish, Bron Wennyly, so named in 1239. It means, Hill of Swallows. A beautiful name. Its sister peak, Roughtor (pronounced Rowter) is not quite so high but on the top of this tor are the remains still of a Chapel dedicated to St. Michael and licensed on 10th November 1535. In 1954 a plaque was erected on the summit to commemorate those who served with the 43rd Wessex Division in the Second World War. The rolling slopes leading down to the river are rich with bronze age huts and stone circles.

To the south east of the moor are East Moor, Hawkstor Downs and Twelve Men's Moor, where Kilmaron Tor and Sharp Tor dominate the skyline. Many people think that Bodmin Moor should still be known by its old name of Fowey (Foy) Moor, for so it was called until about 1773.

After all they argue, and rightly so, Exmoor is named after the River Exe which rises on it, and Dartmoor after the River Dart. There are a number of rivers which rise on Bodmin Moor. To the south of the moor the Trenant, Loveny Dewy and Bedalder and to the north the Henon, Lynher, Camel, Delank and the Fowey. Of them all the Fowey must rank as the largest and the loveliest. Rising on Codda Moor behind Jamaica Inn, it wends its way south through the valley to Golitha Falls, and on and on down until it reaches the sea at Fowey, where it becomes a deep water port, easily navigable by the huge bulk vessels which moor alongside to pick up their cargo of China Clay powder, which is shot straight into their holds.

Running almost completely through wooded valleys, the River Fowey is uniquely beautiful and is reputed to be the river so loved by Kenneth Grahame that he based his wonderful children's classic, "The Wind in the Willows" on it. There are numerous water filled pits on the moors, from old mine workings and quarrying, but the natural highland tarn of Dozmary is among the most famous. About a mile and a half south from Bolventor, it sources the St. Neot river at Three Water's Foot which flows into the Fowey. 1000 ft above sea level and rich in eels, it is a bleak and desolate place. Traces of Palaeolithic and Mesolithic man and Neolithic tombs have been found, and there are still inhabited cottages on its shores.

Golitha Falls, on the river Fowey.
Photograph by Rose Marie Mullins.

Reputedly bottomless, it is in fact, no more than about 4ft deep and has dried out completely on several occasions. Lake of legend, it is supposed to be the lake into which Sir Bedivere threw the magic sword, Excalibur, after Arthur was slain by Mordred at Slaughterbridge. It also supposedly ebbs and flows in tidal fashion and has a whirlpool in its midst.

But the best known legend is that concerning the infamous John Tregeagle. Formerly a 17th Century Steward at Lord Robartes' family home of Lanhydrock, and foster brother to young John Robartes, he was a wicked, covetous man whose crimes, among others, included cheating the Carters of Trevorder, near Wadebridge, out of their lands. He persecuted unmercifully and imprisoned Anne Jefferies, who was an epileptic but widely known and loved for her powers of healing. On Tregeagle's death in 1655, according to Cornish folklore, because of his many sins he was condemned for evermore to balance accounts at night, which were always just sixpence out and to empty the waters of the 'bottomless' Dozmary Pool with a limpet shell with a hole in it! Never more to rest he would sometimes flee to Roche Rock for sanctuary and his loud roars of utter despair could be heard from Dartmoor to Land's End.

Though Cornwall is normally temperate in climate, the high moors are much colder. In the 1880's there was an ice works at Dozmary, near Dozmary cottage. The ice was used to preserve the fish sent from Looe to London. The enclosure to store the ice was cut out of the hillside and paved with granite. Blocks of ice were cut and floated to land and then drawn up a ramp by a horse, and stacked in the enclosure. It was packed tight and covered with peat and transferred in summer by wagon, down the St. Cleer Road, to Liskeard. John Wallace, Vicar of Bodmin, first refers to this road in 1838 as, "The modern road from Jamaica Inn to Liskeard." The ice works closed in the early 1900's.

Before 1844 Bolventor did not exist. There were but four properties in the hamlet itself, and no more than six to eight farms about it. The moors were only just beginning to be cultivated, and people were being encouraged to farm and settle. The Landowner was then Edward Archer and in 1844 he launched his "Bold Venture", the name given to the new farming community for the formation of farms on poor land. The name eventually became Bolventor.

All over the moor there are ancient farmhouses, outbuildings and cottages. Made of granite and slate they stand firm against the elements and the weathering of the years. They have been there so long, the very foundations seem to have grown up out of the soil on which they sit like monstrous grey toadstools, a very part of the earth

Dozmary Cottage shows the site of the Ice Works.
Reproduced by kind permission of the Cornish Studies Library.

beneath them and the landscape around them and one such building, perched high on a hill in the shadow of Tolborough Tor, is Jamaica Inn.

Chapter Two

The Beginning of Jamaica Inn

There is at least one map of Roman roads that shows a road roughly following the present A30 as far as Indian Queens, but later maps do not show it. In 1684 A.K. Hamilton Jenkins conducted a survey of Cornish roads and concluded, "The roads of Cornwall remained for the most part in their primitive state, still following the Highland Ridges, as in ancient times and descend to the valleys by break neck hills, where some river had to be crossed."

The original route from the Polson Bridge that marks the Tamar boundary east of Launceston, across the moor, was but the Norman packhorse track. Goods and passengers were usually sent, or travelled, by sea. John Wesley toured Cornwall no less than thirty-one times between 1743 and 1789, but when he attempted the crossing of, "the great pathless moor", for the first time to reach Bodmin, he found it a daunting experience and only eventually found his way into Bodmin by following the sound of the town's evening curfew bell. Travellers in those days about to embark on the journey across Fowey Moor prudently made their Wills out first!

Until 1716 Launceston had been the seat of the Summer Assizes - due entirely to the bad state of Cornish roads - but then it was decreed that they should also be set up in Bodmin and a signal went out instructing local Magistrates to "make good the way from Launceston, via Camelford and thence to, Bodmin", cutting all trees etc., fit for Coach travel. Their destination was the Royal Coaching Inn at Bodmin, situated where Honey Street meets Mount Folly. There were forty Public Houses in Bodmin at that time. Still there was no attempt made to improve the way across the moor, but in 1754 a Bodmin Innkeeper had direction and distance stones erected along the packhorse way, at quarter of a mile intervals, at his own expense. Elderly residents living in Cardinham and interviewed in the early part of the 19th Century recall the road being built in the 1750's, although it was not completed until the late 1770's.

The road having been at least started, so too must accommodation be built to give shelter and food to the travellers who would use it. Jamaica Inn was built in 1750, for Inns in Cornwall were few and far between before the 17th Century. Initially it stood detached, with four downstairs rooms and five up, including the small room now known as Mary's Room, which was then over the stairs which led straight up from inside the front door. On the left of the Inn as you face it, was a large cow shed, and to the right a row of outhouses and barns. With the Inn went eighty acres of farm land.

The Palmer's Bridge Toll House and the Cottages alongside.
Photograph by Derek French.

By 1770 the new Turnpike Road - authorised from three miles south of Launceston to the Indian Queen's Pub, took the bulk of the mail and passenger traffic to West Cornwall and in 1769 Toll Gates and Toll Houses were installed at Treguddick, Holloway, Two Bridges, Plusha, Palmer's Bridge (at the foot of the hill east of Jamaica Inn) and Callywith. The way then showed as a secondary Turnpike Road until about 1790. In 1773 an amendment to the Public Highways Act stated that, "Cart ways had to be 20' wide and every horse or drift way, 8'. Every tree or shrub to be planted at least 15' from the centre of the road."

With traffic and trade increasing rapidly, in 1778 Jamaica Inn was reconstructed for the first time. The original building was extended widthwise, and the stable block consisting of the coach house, stables and tack room were built onto the front of the cow byre to join up with the Inn, creating the well known L-shaped building that stands today. The Inn was slate hung to disguise the extension and to help weatherproof the building, and two cottages and the row of three farmworkers cottages, each with one room up and one down, were built opposite. The distinctive lintels above the Coach House door and on the cottages, show them to have been built around the same time by the same builder. Four or five miles west of Bolventor stands the old London Inn Coaching House, now known as Pound's-Conce, and this too has the same distinctive lintels. The old Turnpike Road went through Temple on its way to Bodmin, and it was at the London Inn that the Judiciary, on their way to the Assizes, would pull off the Turnpike for two more horses to be added to the team for the last pull into Bodmin. Their Coach was escorted by uniformed, armed and mounted Yeomen

Stage Coaches, Post Chaises and the Mail Coaches came up from Penzance, stopping in Falmouth for the West Indian Mail coming off the Packet boats and made their way eastwards via Inn stages at approximately seven mile intervals. The Norway Inn, Perran Wharf; The Royal Hotel, Truro; The Falmouth Arms, Ladock; The Indian Queens, Goss Moor, Royal Hotel, Bodmin and Jamaica Inn, Bolventor. There were other Inns like the Victoria at Roche, and the London Inn. By 1805 coach journeys from Falmouth to London took only forty-one hours. The King's Head at Five Lanes was also then known as The London Inn, and together with the White Hart at Bodmin was a Coach stage. Jamaica Inn and The Redgates Inn at St. Cleer were Posting Houses. Beer at Jamaica Inn then cost fourpence a quart.

Fast daytime services would demand fourpence to sixpence a mile for those passengers travelling inside the coach and twopence or threepence if they rode up top. The guard blew a three foot long coach horn to give

An aerial view of Bolventor and the Inn in the 1930's, showing the Stannon Clay Works to the left, and the nearness of the coast.

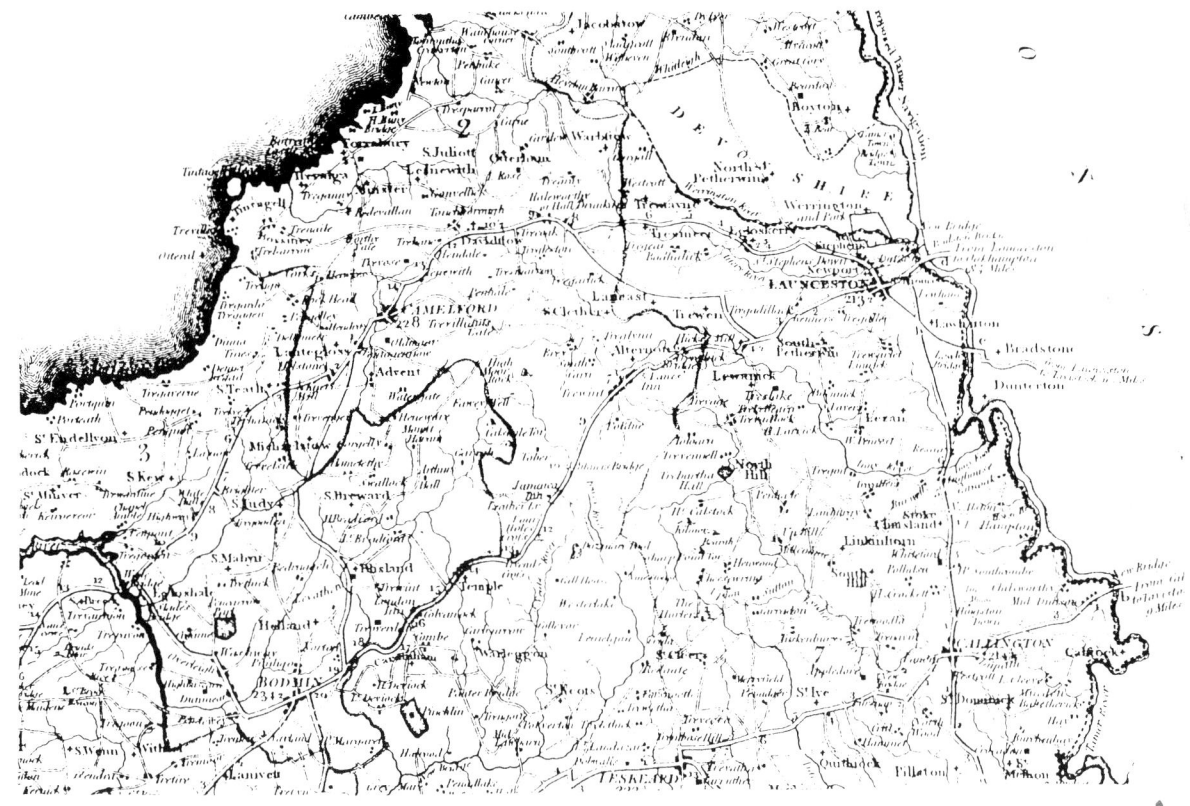

Map printed January 6th 1804, showing Inn on the Secondary Turnpike Road.

warning of their imminent arrival and to clear the road of waggoners and livestock. The horn was blown continuously during fog. Stage Coach passengers of leisure travelled by day and the Mail Coaches usually at night.

In 1842 a traveller by the name of C. Redding stayed at Jamaica Inn and his following description of his stay paints a wonderful portrait of life in the early 19th Century. "The great mail road through Truro and Falmouth, from Launceston, passes through Bodmin and as it was our determination to cross the moors, we mounted the Mail as far as a solitary Inn, situated in a desolate spot, where the Coach changed horses. This Inn is called "The Jamaica Inn". No view is to be obtained on any side, for around were only heathy moors, brown and monotonous. We reached it at nightfall in a drizzling south west rain, and on foot having left the Mail to examine the four hole stone which stands by the roadside, about a mile from the Inn, on a desert heath called Temple Moor, truly a waste, howling wilderness. The Jamaica Inn offered coarse but clean accommodation. During the night the wind swept in gusts across the moors from the south, driving along rain as fine as Vapour." It was in 1798 that John McAdam came to Cornwall to take up the post of Navy Victualling Officer at Falmouth and began to experiment, using Cornish Greenstone as a base for creating new road surfacing materials, which were to eventually transform the roads. During the 19th Century people still had to prise carriage wheels out of the mud ruts with poles.

Cornwall has always been among the poorest of Counties in the British Isles, and still is today. Famous for its ore mining of tin, copper, silver etc., and from 1745 its China Clay, the miners, quarrymen and farmers have always had a very hard life, living with grinding poverty, their working conditions deplorable. Only modern underground miners could possibly begin to comprehend the harshness and danger of their lives. Little wonder then, that smuggling played such an important role for so long, for who could blame such desperate men for taking the opportunity to swell their meagre earnings and improve their lot. Jamaica Inn certainly played its part in smuggling.

Official estimates in the 1780's suggested that half the brandy and a quarter of all tea being smuggled in was landed along the coasts of Cornwall and Devon, and a quarter of all the ships involved in the trade were Devonian or Cornish! Smuggling reached a peak between 1780 and 1840.

There were many ruses to thwart the Preventive Officers. A boat out to sea waiting to land cargo, could be warned in many ways. Watching one particular field, for example, a man seen riding a white horse would signal the all clear, but if he were on foot it would indicate that the coast was not clear to land.

Much has been made by readers of the novel "Jamaica Inn" about the fact that the Inn is not on the coast but miles inland and it could not, therefore, they scoff, possibly have been involved in smuggling. The novel of course, is more about Wreckers than Smugglers, but the Inn most certainly was involved in smuggling. By today's roads the ways to the coasts, either north or south, are indeed tortuous and long, but the old pack animal tracks that went directly across the moors and the secret ways known only to local men, were little more than a dozen or so miles from Looe and Polperro to the south, and Trebarwith, Tintagel and Boscastle to the north. Booty could be sunk, with markers, waiting for the chance to pick up. It could be stored in a Vugga (or Vouggha - Cornish Cave), then hauled up the cliff if necessary, barrels and packages strapped to a man's back and even carried on foot a mile or two inland before being loaded onto packhorses, or transported in an obliging farmer's wagon. The goods were smuggled from France and Ireland in Irish Wherries - the small, shallow draught sailing vessels. The Inn, far away from prying eyes and isolated, was a regular stopping point for the contraband en route into Devon, and onwards up country. It also did a considerable trade in rum and there are those who think that this trade was how Jamaica Inn obtained its unusual name. It has been said, from time to time, that the Inn was at some point or other known as the New Inn, but it has not been possible to confirm this, nor can I see any reason why it should be so called. The King's Head at Five Lanes was definitely known as the New Inn at some point in it's history and maybe that is where the confusion arises.

Jamaica Inn was most certainly known as that in 1789 and it is almost equally certain that it was so named in honour of the Trelawney family (sometimes spelt Trelawny), who were then very important landowners in the area. The Manor of Trelawne, original seat of the Trelawney family, lay to the north of Altarnun and the land that they owned included the Bolventor area. Sir John Trelawney was a distinguished military man in the reign of Henry V, and was a firm favourite of the King. Over the gates of the old walled town of Launceston were the Arms of Henry V and a quote that read, "He that will aught for mee, Let him love well Sir John Tirlawnee." (Trelawney). The Barton of Tre-lawn-y (i.e. The Oak Grove Town), stood in the Parish of the Hundreds of Lesnewth as did the Inn, until it passed into other hands due to the lack of male heirs, and the house was eventually demolished. Much of its stones and wood were used in the renovation of the Church at Altarnun.

Two of the distinguished members of the family were Governors of Jamaica. Edward Trelawny, 4th son of Sir Jonathan Trelawny, was Governor from 1738 - 1754 and his Governorship was particularly effective. He died in 1756 and Sir William Trelawny became Governor in 1766 and he died in Jamaica in 1772. Since Edward Trelawny was still Governor in 1750 when the Inn was first built and opened, it was undoubtedly so named Jamaica Inn from the beginning. There could be no reason to change it at any later stage. Any advertisements or articles appearing in newspapers from 1789 to the present day refer to the Inn as Jamaica Inn, and so, too, do the old maps on which it appears.

CHAPTER THREE

Early Owners and Landlords

The Inn has changed ownership many times since it was built and - as Deeds held by the current owners do not go back very far - it has not been possible to trace all the former owners. However, from the time that the Inn was first built up until 1946, it was run by tenants only, under the direct landownership or that of the lessee.

In 1784 a ninety-nine year lease was drawn up between Admiral William Langdon and John Broad, (described as an Innkeeper) and this included Dryworks Plantation, east of Jamaica Inn, the Lower Park on Symons Ham and Shepherds Hill, Altarnun, as well as the area now known as Bolventor. The following year, from the title, "Lease and Release", for £350 property again changed hands, registered as follows, "From Elias Lang of Tredethy, St. Mabyn, to Sir John Morshead of Trenant Park, Blisland, all that part of the Manor of St. Neot, consisting of Redmoor in St. Neot, Tolborough - or Trewint - Moor and Wett Hill in St. Neot, Altarnun, Blisland and St. Breward, late in occupation of George Devonshire, now of James Broad - Innkeeper". By this time John Broad had taken tenancy of the Inn at Five Lanes, and James Broad was the Innkeeper of Jamaica. He died in 1803 and his Estate included horses, colts and mules worth £70, and chattels worth £205. His widow Elizabeth continued tenancy of the Inn until 1828. On the 30th September of the year 1828, an indenture was made between James West Esq., of Bryanstone Square, Middlesex, on the first part (possibly a Solicitor) and Francis Hearle Rodd of Trebartha Hall, of the second part, and John King Lethbridge Esq., of Tregeare, of the third part. Still then in the ownership of the Morsheads, the indenture reads, "Dame Elizabeth Morshead, a widow, sells to Francis H. Rodd, Trewint Moor, Withiel and other lands containing by estimation 1,565 acres together with a certain messuage and tenement commonly called, or known, by the name of Jamaica Inn, situate in the Parish of Altarnun, in the County of Cornwall, late in the tenure of, or occupation of James Broad and now of Elizabeth Broad, Widow, all for £700." Thus the whole estate, including the Inn, passed into the ownership of the Rodd family of Trebartha Hall, North Hill.

The ancient estate of Trebartha was given to a Norman Knight by William the Conqueror, and the noble Knight took Trebartha as his family name, but by 1498, the line of male heirs was exhausted, so Anna Trebartha married one Thomas Spoure, and the Spoure family held the estate until 1729 when the family again ran out of male heirs. The heiress, Mary Spoure, was affianced to her cousin Francis Rodd when she died of smallpox, but she had willed the Trebartha Estate to her cousin and thus, after two hundred and thirty years, the Trebartha Estate passed out of the Spoure family.

By the time that the Rodds bought the 1,565 acres which included the Inn from Dame Elizabeth Morshead, they had been powerful, influential landowners for a hundred years but they did not long continue to be outright owners of Jamaica Inn. In 1846 most of the lands and properties bought from the Morsheads were sold on with ninety-nine year leases and the Tithe Map of 1841, which apportioned the value of land quality to enable the Church to take a tenth (Tithe) of the produce of the land to upkeep "rates", shows that the "Bold Venture" Landowner was then one Edward Archer, under the ninety-nine year lease scheme, though the name of Francis Rodd still appears. Back in 1790 Edward Archer had also purchased part of the Manor called Gunnon, Tregarlick (or Tre-garrick) and Trelawne - the ancient Trelawny Manor. The information found on the Tithe map records states that the tenants at that time of the Inn, were John Langstone and Thomas Dunn. A report in the Sherborne Mercury on 11th September 1835 shows, "an assault by a man named Wilton, Keeper of the turnpike gate at Palmer's Bridge, on Mrs Dunn, the Landlord's wife." In September 1843 Thomas Dunn advertised that the Posting House (The Inn) was again being refitted to encourage more Coach trade. In 1846 Squire Rodd built the Bolventor Church, which is situated down in the hollow to the north west of the Inn, (now the other side of the dual carriageway), and also the cottage style Parsonage House. He also had built the original village school - The National School - which is now the village Reading Room, just west of the Jamaica Cottages. Bolventor became a separate Parish when the Church was consecrated.

It was consecrated on July 3rd 1848 and dedicated to The Holy Trinity, seated two hundred worshippers and cost Squire Rodd £666. The population of Bolventor was then three hundred and forty-four. The first Baptism, of the Toll House gatekeeper's daughter, Fanny Weale, took place on 10th September 1848; the first marriage in June 1849 and the first burial in 1850.

William Medland followed Thomas Dunn as Innkeeper of the Jamaica Inn and he was followed in 1858 by John Colwill, who straightway contradicted the rumour that he, "was not going to take Hunting Parties as usual." The Inn had been well used as a Sportsmen's Resort since 1840. Mr Colwill advertised the Inn as, "accommodating Hunting Parties, and having well aired beds and good stabling". Yet more reconstruction work took place in his tenancy which ended in September 1871, the Inn being then described as, "with seventeen rooms, of which eight were bedrooms." A further entry in the 1859 edition of

Murray's Landbook for Travellers states, "This Inn is frequented by Sportsmen in the winter, and affords comfortable though somewhat rude accommodation." Squire Rodd and his descendants were very keen Huntsmen, and it has long been the tradition of Jamaica Inn to accommodate the local Hunts, as they still do to this day.

William Mason became the next known tenant, and he was fined in 1876 for allowing sheep with scab to stray. After him came one Sergeant Courtney Doidge. Mr and Mrs Hawkes took over the lease next, but Mr Hawkes died in 1879 and his wife Mary became the lessee. By then however, great changes had taken place in Cornwall due to the fervent spread and strength of Methodism. Alcohol was frowned upon and from February 1880 the decree was that the Inn premises were to be let once more, but, "not thence-forth to be used as an Inn." It was known as The Jamaica Inn Temperance Hotel. Mary Hawke was assisted during her tenancy by joint Landlords Francis Bray and W.P. Chegwin. They were there when the great blizzard of 1895 made the road impassable for days. The Inn remained a temperance hotel until the second World War. In 1896 an Act of Parliament was passed to allow motor cars to use roads and so, passing into the 20th Century, Jamaica Inn faced the beginning of another significant phase in its history.

It did not happen overnight. For another fifty years little changed at the Inn itself, only the modes of transport bringing the travellers to its threshold. Until 1945 it stayed firmly rooted in the past, happy in its isolation, harbouring the souls of the men, women and children who had lived, worked and played beneath its slate roof, and within it's granite walls for so many years, each one leaving something of themselves to be absorbed into its timbers, though some of the souls, it would seem, had not gone to rest.

CHAPTER FOUR

From Ghoulies and Ghosties

Until I was about thirty years old there was no greater sceptic than myself with regard to Ghoulies and Ghosties and Long Leggety Beasties. I regarded with a kind of

pitying scorn anyone who believed in such things, and thought them soft in the head or endowed with an over active imagination until - that is - I had an 'experience'

myself for which there was no logical or reasonable explanation and for which I could not doubt the evidence of my own eyes. Nowadays I freely admit that there are indeed more things in Heaven and Earth than we will ever know and I, for one, would never again say that there are no such things as ghosts.

Cornwall abounds with ghostly tales, in keeping with its mystical nature. The moor, with its silent sentinels of stone, its mists and bewitching sense of timelessness invites such stories. Who is to say how many of them, if any, are true?

On the 14th April 1844, which was Easter Sunday, Charlotte Dymond, the eighteen year old flighty maid-servant of Widow Phillipa Peter, of Penhale Farm, in the Inny Valley on Davidstow Moor, was murdered upon the moor at the foot of Roughtor. Her throat had been cut - twice - but her body was not found until nine days after she had gone missing. It was found in Advent Parish, on the right bank of Roughtor Ford. Her co-worker, Matthew Weekes, in his early twenties, lame in one leg and illiterate, was at once the prime suspect as the foul murderer, as he had been courting Charlotte who was said to have tired of him. After being questioned by Police and before her body was found, he ran away and was traced to Plymouth, where his sister lived, and was arrested on the Hoe by Constable Bennett. By 27th April he was incarcerated in the grim Bodmin Goal, which had been built in 1779. Belief of his guilt was unanimous.

On 30th July a Coach and six, escorted by a uniformed Sheriff's Troop, carried Mr Justice Wightman and Mr Justice Patteson past Jamaica Inn from Exeter to Bodmin for Matthew Weekes' trial, which took place on Friday 2nd August at Bodmin Assize Court. Matthew was found guilty, not to anyone's great surprise, and he was condemned to death. The unfortunate man was duly hanged on Monday 12th August at Bodmin Goal. It was a Public hanging. His body was left to hang for the usual one hour and one minute and then removed to be buried in the precincts of the prison, either the prison garden or the coal yard. Jamaica Inn and the other Inns and Taverns in and around Bodmin must have heartily welcomed such executions, for they were well attended! Twenty thousand good souls were present at Matthew's hanging and the town did brisk business for three days with market stalls being set up in the streets. The last public hanging there was in 1863.

Although he confessed, subsequent thorough investigations, (including a reconstruction of the case, broadcast from Pebble Mill on Macleod's Mysteries in January 1978), have cast considerable doubt on his guilt and there was even a strong case mounted for a verdict of suicide, in spite of the method used. The ghost of Charlotte Dymond is still said to haunt the moor.

The poor girl was seen by the source of the River Alan (tributary to the Camel) in the early twentieth century by members of the Callington 5th Corps - The Cornwall Rifle Volunteers - whilst on night duty and they refused to keep further watch. At the end of the 19th century, some of the tough, hardy, down to earth Stannon clayworkers also reported sightings. In the 1970's two men out with a dog were climbing Roughtor one day, when the dog became very excited, running to and fro with its tail between its legs, behaving in a very agitated fashion. It suddenly refused to go any further and hid in a cranny. The owner carried the dog back down fearing it to be ill, but as soon as he put it back on the ground it scampered off as if nothing had happened.

Charlotte Dymond was buried in an unmarked grave in the Churchyard of Davidstow Church and a monument was erected to her memory, near the place where her body was found. It was paid for by subscriptions from local people. It could be said, however, that if she DID commit suicide that may well be the reason why her ghost still walks and she is unable to rest, for - if it WAS suicide - an innocent man was hanged. Charlotte lies buried in consecrated ground, and in those days suicides had to be buried at night in unconsecrated ground, without the usual religious ceremonies. They also had to

The Memorial Stone to Charlotte Dymond set up on the moor below Roughtor.
Photograph by Peter Mullins.

Roughtor Ford where Charlotte's body was found.
Photograph by Peter Mullins.

wait over fourteen years before being allowed to be buried in a Churchyard, and then with no Service. Nor were executed people allowed to be buried in consecrated soil and thus their pole positions were reversed. The truth will never be known. Behind the Inn lies a lovely little meadow, known as Scaddick Hill Meadow. Nothing has ever been seen there, but few people would use it and all who did felt exactly the same - that they were not alone. Derek French was one of the men, then living at Blackhill Farm, near Codda Ford, who would regularly cross the meadow and he freely admits that he never did so without instinctively looking back over his shoulder, sensing another's presence, and tells how one of the village women who cleaned for Mrs Bray at Blackhill, had to be met and escorted through the meadow on her way to her work and back again.

Jamaica Inn has its share of ghosts, and is most certainly haunted by at least one man. Many years ago a stranger stood at the old bar drinking his ale. He was called outside and departed leaving his ale on the bar counter. He did not return and the following morning his murdered body was found out on the moor. The murder remained a total mystery, but in 1911 there was a great deal of interest and correspondence in the local press concerning a strange man seen by many people, sitting on the wall outside the Inn. He did not move, or speak, even when spoken to and his appearance was uncannily like that of the murdered man.

One of our main sources of information about the Inn and its recent history, is Reg Carthew, and more will be said of him later on in this book. In the sixty years that he has been associated with the Inn he has experienced many things. We asked him very seriously about the Inn and the supposed hauntings and he eventually told us that he truly does believe the Inn to be haunted. He said that whenever he had to go to what was the old engine room, to the back east end of the Inn, that - as he lifted his hand to the bolt - he always automatically looked over his shoulder feeling someone was standing behind him and that one day Mr Grose, who was Manager of the Inn in the early fifties, spoke to him hesitantly, asking - with a somewhat sheepish look - if he (Reg) had ever 'felt anything' when he went to the engine room door? He seemed both relieved and apprehensive when Reg told of the sensation he always experienced there and Mr Grose (former Household Cavalry and no faint heart) shamefacedly admitted that he, too, sensed a presence.

Mr Palmer, one of the owners of the Inn after the War - the only one ever to live there with his family - also saw a ghost. The family frequently heard footsteps on the stairs when there was no one about and one evening as Reg and Mr Palmer were seated on two settles in the old stock room by a fire which was refusing to burn, about to each light up a cigarette and talking together, Mr Palmer - with a muttered curse - suddenly leapt to his feet, his cigarettes and lighter falling to the floor, and shot across the room towards the outer door as Reg watched in amazement. When he returned he furiously asked if Reg had seen where the man had gone. But Reg had seen no one. When Reg stayed at the Inn, as he often has done over the years, he used one of the bedrooms over the Joss Merlyn Bar, in the part of the building that had been added onto the Inn in 1788. The only toilets then in the Inn were at the far western end of the passage downstairs, and whenever he had to leave his room and cross over into the older part of the Inn, night or day, he would experience a feeling of penetrating coldness, chilling his body to the bone. Mr and Mrs Duffy, managers in the sixties also reported hearing footsteps going up the back stairs.

In more recent times, one of the cooks who has worked for many years at the Inn, was waiting on the managers who were having their lunch in the Stable Bar, which leads into the Restaurant. The place was empty apart from themselves, but she saw a green cloaked man come through from the restaurant and go out towards reception. Puzzled she asked the Manager who the man was? He replied, in astonishment, "What man?" "The one who has just come out of the restaurant," she answered. The manager stared at her. "The restaurant door is locked," he said. And so it was. Two of the waitresses a few years ago were also frightened by unexplained happenings in the restaurant. Having finished laying up for breakfast one evening, long after the diners had all left, one of them returned to check that she had put clean ashtrays round, only to find that she had but that one of them contained a smouldering cigarette. The following evening she could again smell cigarette smoke after the restaurant had been cleaned and tidied, and called her colleague to see if she, too, could smell anything. They not only both smelled the cigarette but saw a spiral of smoke rising from nowhere.

In early December of 1996, my husband and I had to call a plumber in to replace the pump on our Baxi Boiler central heating system. He was very talkative, and my husband mentioned to him that I was in the dining room, working on this book and had reached the Chapter on ghosts. The man told us both that he had worked several times in the sixties at the Inn, going up into the loft to work on piping and the two large water tanks which were up there. "I never saw anything," he said, "but I always remember that I used to make my way over to the tanks and look back longingly to the trap door. I hated being up there and could not wait to get down." The tanks were to the east of the loft!

Chapter five

Bolventor

Up until the last decade Bolventor was always a very close knit community, with daily life centering around the farms, Jamaica Inn, the Church and Chapel. Its people were hardworking and friendly. In 1878 a new school was built in Bolventor, and it opened the following year with ninety-five children. It was known as The Board School -later the County Primary School and for a long time its pupils ranged from infants to school leavers.

Church and Chapel were well attended, particularly the Chapel. The original Chapel of St. Luke's was planted on the Dozmary track in the 12th Century, suppressed by the Chantries Act and desecrated at the Reformation. The Norman font was removed to the new Church of St. Luke, Tideford, in the 1840's. There is now nothing left of this ancient Chapel, the remains are thought to be under the courtyard of St. Luke's farm on the Dozmary Road. The new St. Luke's Chapel was built on the St. Cleer Road in 1891.

The Friends of St. Luke's were founded in 1892 and every year on the Sunday and Monday nearest to Midsummer Day, anniversary celebrations were held. There were open air services at the Chapel, to accommodate the hundreds attending. This was followed on the Monday by an open air picnic at Dozmary. The people would arrive in their masses, on foot and horseback and in carriages and wagons, with lanterns to light their way home. The Procession would follow a brass band and march under the Banner of "St. Luke's Bible Christian Sunday School" down to the lake. There a huge picnic was spread, with water boiling over turf fires for tea. Boat trips on the lake were organised, with a hired boat from Looe - the only time boating was ever allowed on Dozmary. There were solos, recitations and community singing, followed by an evening Service. This very popular event carried on for nearly eighty years and was only cancelled in very bad weather. From 1965 to 1974 no picnic was held because of the weather and the anniversary celebrations ceased soon after that.

Children's sportsdays were also held at Dozmary in one of the big fields belonging to the Inn, known as Eight Acres or Big Run, as were Gymkhanas and the Bolventor Horticultural Shows, which started in 1933 and finished in 1939. Major E.S. Rodd (the last surviving male member of the Rodd family) was the President and lunches were held at the Inn, sometimes also presided over by Captain Morshead, from Blisland. The East Cornwall Hounds and the Bolventor Harriers (formed in 1949), also met in the Inn Courtyard, and both Hunts still hold Meets there today.

St. Luke's Methodist Church's Annual Picnic at Dozmary Pool.
Photographs reproduced by kind permission of the Cornish Studies Library.

The refreshment tent.
Photograph loaned by Derek French.

Bolventor Harriers meet at Berrio Bridge, river Lybner, near North Hill.
Reproduced by kind permission of the Cornish Studies Library.

In 1923 land, stone and labour was offered by landowners and farmers for transformation of the track from St. Neot to Bolventor into a Parish road, the Council agreeing to maintain it. It was formally opened and celebrated in conjunction with St. Luke's annual tea.

In 1923 Bert Horrell came to the Inn as Tenant Landlord, and it was during his tenancy in November 1930, that Daphne Du Maurier visited the Inn for the first time. Daphne Du Maurier was born in London in 1907, the second daughter of Muriel and Gerald Du Maurier, a very famous Actor/Manager of his day. Born into a talented theatrical and artistic family, she was blessed with a vivid imagination and a desire to write. This desire was fuelled even more by her immediate love for Cornwall, after her parents purchased a holiday home here, at Boddinick, overlooking the River Fowey.

It was whilst staying at Boddinick that she wrote her first successful novel "The Loving Spirit", which was published in 1931. She went on to become one of the most successful authors ever. Most of her work is still in print and sells as well today as it ever did. The gift shop at Jamaica Inn does brisk business in the sale of her books, which are as popular as ever. She wrote a total of thirty-eight books including Rebecca, The King's General, Frenchman's Creek, The Birds and - of course - Jamaica Inn, which was published in 1936. Daphne spent as much of her time in Cornwall as she could and became very friendly with author Sir Arthur Quiller Couch, known as "Q", who lived across the water in Fowey and his daughter Foy, (named after the original spelling of Fowey). Both Daphne and Foy enjoyed horseriding and they went together to spend a few days at Jamaica Inn, which was then still a temperance house, to ride on the moors. The story goes that they set off in the early afternoon on horseback, to visit an elderly lady living on the Trebartha Estate and their way took them south-east across East Moor towards Hawkstor Downs. Bad weather closed in with mist and rain and they got hopelessly lost. They dismounted and took shelter for a time in a derelict cottage but - in the end - tired, wet and dispirited they wisely decided to give the horses their head and hope that they would find their own way back. It says much for horse sense that the riders did eventually, and with great relief, see the tall chimneys of Jamaica Inn rising up before them and an anxious Landlord, Bert Horrell, out with lanterns to begin a search. Her first view of the old Inn and this experience left a lasting impression on Daphne Du Maurier of the inhospitable moors and sowed the seed in her fertile imagination for the story that is "Jamaica Inn". The rest - as they say - is history.

Dame Daphne Du Maurier.
Photographed by her son, Christian Browning, during her work on "Vanishing Cornwall".

Still from the video of Jamaica Inn, with Jane Seymour as Mary and Patrick McGoohan as Joss Merlyn.
Made by ATV in 1983.

Published in 1936 it was her first real commercial success and, together with Rebecca, is probably one of her best known works. Several of her stories were transferred to the screen including Rebecca, My Cousin Rachel, Frenchman's Creek, The Birds, Don't Look Now and Jamaica Inn. Two films have been made so far of Jamaica Inn and a third is possibly in the offing. The first Hollywood version was like most Hollywood versions of good books, it bore so little resemblance to the original story as to be best forgotten. The much later film, for television, starring Jane Seymour as Mary, Trevor Eve as Jem and Patrick McGoohan as the evil Landlord, Joss Merlyn, was an altogether more realistic portrayal, though much of it was filmed out of Cornwall.

It has been very fortunate for subsequent owners and landlords of Jamaica Inn that, when Daphne Du Maurier first wrote her brilliant novel about wreckers and smugglers, the romance of the Inn's unusual name induced her to retain it for the title and story, for from the time of it's publication onwards, the devotees of Daphne Du Maurier have flocked to the Inn in ever increasing numbers and have ensured not only it's survival but also its continuing prosperity. At this time, before the outbreak of World War II, the house opposite the Inn, known today as the Jamaica Inn Farmhouse, was the Smithy and also the village Post Office. Reg Carthew well remembers taking horses up to Bolventor to be shod by Bill Burrows, the blacksmith. Village life was then complete.

In 1938 the Rodd family finally sold the 2,300 acres in and around Bolventor to a local Auctioneer and Estate Agent, Walter Dennis, though still with the proviso that any sale of land, even for building, must still include rights of way for hunting. Thus the selling off of the individual properties, land and farms, including the Inn, inevitably began. The day of the great landowners in the area was over.

A. Reddicliffe - Postman on his rounds.

Jamaica Inn in the 1950's before any modern building, showing clearly the path to the moor between Inn and Calf Shed.
Photograph loaned by Derek French.

Jamaica Inn in the 1930's before the renovations begun by Stanley Thomas.

The Inn in the late forties.
Reproduced by kind permission of the Cornish Studies Library.

Chapter Six

The War Years

Reg Carthew began his long association with the Inn during the mid 1930's. His father, Ernest John Carthew, was the Captain of the Clay Mine beneath Hawks Tor, some three miles west of Bolventor. The mine was owned by Bowaters. China Clay mining had begun on the moor in 1860. The clay was pumped from the pit into settling tanks. It was then piped from the tanks passing underneath the road to Temple Hill and continued on its way through the pipe system down to the A38 Bodmin road by natural gravity and for eighteen miles to its terminal on the south coast.

The young Reg would come up to the Inn on a Sunday morning with his father and he recalls actually meeting one of the old coach drivers who had driven the horse drawn coaches up from Penzance to the Inn and back, before 1910. Reg was at the Inn on the morning that war was declared. During the war he served in the RAF, and spent a lot of that wartime service in Rhodesia in Training Command. He was repatriated in 1946. Bert Horrell's tenancy came to an end in 1939 and Reg's father bought up all the Inn stock when Mr Horrell left. Mr Horrell was succeeded as landlord by Claude Finnamore, who was at the Inn for the duration of the war until 1945 when Walter Dennis sold the Inn to Stanley Thomas, a Plymouth businessman. Mr Thomas was the first of the post-war absentee owners.

After the war Reg went back to the Inn, where he worked on and off for many years. He now lives down on the Lizard, but is still called on from time to time by the owners of the Inn whenever there is a problem with the old workings of the building, recognition being given to his vast store of knowledge about Jamaica Inn. Jack of all trades he was the general factotum, invaluable help, an asset to the business. He knew Major Rodd very well, and chauffered his sister about on many occasions, knowing well the old Trebartha Hall. He did have several other occupations whilst working at the Inn, including helping out at the Drum Major Club in Bodmin, which had been the old Hospital of the Duke of Cornwall's Light Infantry Barracks. In that role he sported a different 'uniform' every evening and was quite a character.

During the ownership of the Inn by William and Margaret Palmer, (1962 - 1964), he had one of the saddest experiences of his life. Flight Lt. Beer was Reg's old Station Adjutant in Rhodesia. He had been a good officer whom Reg not only looked up to but was also very fond of. Working one day outside the Inn on Mr Palmer's car, Reg suddenly spotted his old Officer entering the Inn. He

Reg Carthew serving in the bar in the 60's.
Photograph kindly lent by David Smith.

made haste towards the door hoping to have words with the man he had thought so highly of, to thank him for the many past kindnesses, but was ordered back outside by the Palmers' son and to this day he has never forgotten it, or ceased to regret the lost opportunity, as Mr Beer died not long after. Neither has Reg forgotten 1973, when the 30' caravan he was working in at Jamaica Inn, was somersaulted three times in severe gale force winds, coming to rest 25' away and from which he emerged totally unharmed!

Reg has seen a long line of Owners and Managers come and go during his years at the Inn, his stories are very funny and - mostly - unrepeatable! One such tale involved the wife of one of the Landlords who was deeply involved in an illicit relationship with a local farmer. A light would be placed in a strategic window of the Inn by the lady when the coast was clear and shortly afterwards a horse would be found discreetly tethered at the back of the Inn, usually at milking time when the farmer's wife would have been left to do the milking!

Reg's brother, Maurice, also worked at Hawks Tor Clay Works, and his great-cousin, Emma Nottle, was a much loved character in the village of Bolventor. Emma was a widow who lived in the far end cottage of the row of three - known as Jamaica Cottages - across the road to the west of the Inn. She somehow started a small shop there in 1921, with ten shillings - all the money that she had in the world - and made it a success. She also did teas and even advertised lodgings, though with just one room down and one room up and a lean-to extension on the back, goodness only knows where the lodger stayed! In 1939 Joseph Giles, aged 82, visiting relatives in the area, partook of a cup of tea in Mrs Nottle's tea room and romance blossomed. Emma - who by then was 78 years old with 3 children, 18 grandchildren and 23 great grandchildren - and Joseph were married by the Reverend Kneebone, in Bolventor Church. The Reporter from the Cornish Times who was sent to cover the great occasion, found himself standing in for both the best man (who failed to turn up) and the bellringer, who was indisposed.

The Couch family, who lived in the middle cottage next door, also opened a small shop in competition, selling tobacco and Emma and Mrs Couch were frequently heard outside the rival businesses in heated altercation. As if Emma's commitments were not enough, she took on a foster child, little Joyce Hambley, after her mother died very young and Emma raised the child. The Hambleys lived at outer Priddacombe, near Butter's Tor and their lives were bleak indeed. It wasn't unusual for them to find adders asleep in their boots in the mornings, the snakes having been attracted by the warmth.

Reg Carthew wearing one of the 'uniforms' he used during his work at the "Drum Major" Pub, Ex-Bodmin Barracks.

Chris Skinner and Maurice Carthew in the Engine Room at the Hawks Tor Clay Works, late 50's, and the two Ruston Hornsby Diesel Engines.

Treviscoe Pit - Washing out the Raw Clay.   *Goonvean Pit - Old Beam Engine at work.*
Reproduced by kind permission of the Cornish Studies Library.

Jamaica Cottages in the 1920's.

Emma Nottle and her foster daughter, Joyce Hambley, outside Emma's shop in Jamaica Cottages.

Emma Nottle outside her shop in the Jamaica Cottages and the shop set up in opposition next door, by Mr and Mrs Couch.

When War began, the whole of the moor played as important a part as anywhere else in the British Isles. The Post Office moved into the Inn (to where the children's room is now), and it was also used as an Estate Office for the English China Clay Lovering Estate, where local farmers came to pay their rents. Having begun to sell off the lands that he had previously owned, Major E. Stanhope Rodd of Trebartha also began in 1940 to sell off parts of the Trebartha Estate, as he had but four daughters and no male heir to follow him. Brian Latham, travelling down to view the 500 acres of mature woodlands he had seen advertised for sale, fell in love with the beauty of the estate, which was then some 4,000 acres, and he eventually bought the whole of Trebartha. During the War the big house was requisitioned, as were so many others, and used to accommodate some of the 8,000 American Troops stationed in the area on the moor, from 1942. The Hall was left in such a dilapidated condition after the war that it had to be demolished, and a new house was built in its place.

Derek French came to Bolventor in October 1940 with his Mother to escape the bombing in Hastings, where the family lived. Initially they came to stay with relatives, but then Mrs French decided to stay for a while and they moved into the Bolventor Vicarage, sharing the Vicarage with the Revd. Craig. The young Derek began to help out on some of the outlying farms for something to do, and eventually he moved in with Mr and Mrs Bray on Blackhill Farm, below Codda Downs, while his Mother went back to Hastings. Mr Bray was a well know local water diviner. Derek's work was hard and varied and included peat cutting. Most farms and the Inn had turf cutting rights on Minzies Downs, south west of the A30 at Bolventor, and almost everyone burned peat for fuel. Surface vegetation would be cut and removed with slitting and butting knives and the peat below was lifted with a turf iron into slabs about 3" thick, 9" wide and 2' long. These were left on the moor to dry and had to be turned regularly to assist the drying process. It was then brought off the moor by horse and cart and stood in peat stacks, near to the homestead. A "Journey" was 2,000 turves. As a fuel it was very efficient. Part of the peat moor at Smallacombe Downs caught fire many years ago and was just left to burn. It smouldered for a whole year until it burnt right down to the granite.

Mrs Phyllis Best, who spent most of her life in Bolventor, recalls the Bolventor men who worked at Stannon Clay quarry below Roughtor, walking the five and a half miles to work each morning, and on their return stopping to cut 1,000 turves on Priddacombe Downs, which she used to go out to 'turn'. She remembers her mother cooking over peat fires. The baking iron - flat and round - was heated thoroughly over the turf fire and then removed. The full round baking dishes were put on the hot plate,

Peatcutters near Brown Willy.

A wagon of turves, Derek French and Ben on top, Polish refugee and Mrs Bertha Chegwyn.
Photograph loaned by Derek French.

A welcome break from peat cutting. Derek French, 4th from right and Averil Sleep (later to become his wife) next to him with her parents.
Photograph kindly loaned by Derek French.

and an upturned metal bowl placed over the top to seal it. The hot turves were then heaped up over the bowl and this cooked to perfection the food inside. Mrs Best's great-grand-father, William Perry, married Frances Jane Colwill, the daughter of John Colwill - who was the Innkeeper of Jamaica Inn - on 15th March 1859 and her grandfather was born in Mary's room, over the porch. He became the first Policeman in Bolventor.

Bodmin Moor was in continual use for Army exercises and King George VI visited Bolventor on his way to Camelford, to observe one such exercise. He stayed for lunch which was held in a big marquee in one of the fields. On one occasion the big guns were being fired from Brown Gelly - to the south of the Inn, near Park China Clay Works - to Brown Willy - to the north of the Inn - and the American Troops were advancing towards Brown Willy, close behind the barrage. Four live shells fell short amidst the men but, by some miracle, one man having the heel of his boot blown off proved to be the only casualty sustained!

Farming on the moors in the 1940's.
Photographs loaned by Derek French.

Farming on the moors in the 1940's.
Photographs loaned by Derek French.

The farmers were always notified in advance of any exercise and would have plenty of time to go out and round up their stock, but Derek French was out one day on horse-back, looking for one more cow that was missing on Codda Tor, when a shell landed just the other side of the Tor. The horse bucked, the girth snapped and the saddle flew up and away, lifting Derek with it. Somehow he managed to keep his seat as the horse bolted home and Derek had to return later to find the saddle.

He was working on the moor with Les Chegwyn and Mr Gardner of North Tober one day, when a Seafire from St. Merryn Royal Naval Air Station crashed in thick fog and in flames, at Codda Farm behind the Inn. The men were first on the scene. They found only the torso of the pilot, still on fire, and noticed something hard in the tunic pocket. They managed to recover the object and found photographs of the pilot's wife and children inside.

A number of planes came down in the immediate area during the War. One German Bomber crashed on Brown

The Home Guard for the Bolventor area. **Front row:** *1st left: Joe Janes, 2nd left: Les Chegwyn, 3rd left: Frank Sleep, 7th left: George Smeeth.* **Middle row:** *3rd left: Tommy Hooper (alias, Blackbird), 2nd right: Norman Harper.* **Back row:** *Arthur Stevens, 5th left: Sam Sleep.*

Willy and the crew were buried immediately on the hill in unmarked graves. A Blenheim Bomber hit Brown Willy's south slope. The fuselage was found there and the engines the other side of the hill. A Stirling Bomber crashed on Bray Down, but the crew managed to bale out and a Beaufort also crash-landed on top of Palmer's Bridge Hill in the middle of the night. One of the worst incidents was in 1945 when an RAF Halifax crashed, killing all on board. Working out on the moor one day Derek French watched a Tank Exercise come to similar grief. He was approached by the Tank Commanding Officer and asked for directions to High Moor. The C.O. was very strongly advised by Derek to do a detour, as the land between Codda and High Moor was a bog, known as High Moor Marsh. "Nonsense" the Officer boasted, signalling back and waving his men on. "These tanks will go through anything!" They are still at the bottom of the bog, though the men inside did manage to scramble clear.

On another occasion Charlie Lee, a somewhat simple man who did occasional work at the Inn, was on the Moor near Catshole Downs when the Hunt appeared. The Huntsman reined in, nodded towards the bog between Catshole and Priddacombe and asked Charlie, "Is there a bottom to that one, boy?" "Ais" said Charlie. So in they went. They got bogged down and hounds, horses and men struggled out, the Huntsman incandescent with rage. Purple faced he thundered at his seemingly dim-witted informant. "I thought you said there was a bottom to that!" "Ais" a poker featured Charlie answered. "Yoom 'adn't fan'd 'un yit." Possibly Charlie preferred the four legged predators to the two legged, and wasn't so simple after all. The Reading Room in Bolventor (formerly the village school) was the centre for the meetings of the Home Guard and almost every part of the moor was in use during the war including Davidstow where an airfield was built, mainly for the American Heavy Bombers sent on daylight raids into Germany, but it proved to be a singularly bad choice of location. Davidstow was so frequently fog-bound that it was of little real use, and was used no more after 1945.

The build up of Americans intensified as they prepared for Omaha and the Normandy Landings and Claude Finnamore had as one of his guests at the Inn, General Patton, who stayed there for a few days before setting off with his Troops on D-Day. Claude cooked the breakfast that morning for his distinguished guest, using twelve eggs that the General had supplied himself.

Claude Finnamore was a very good Organist and gave music lessons whilst at the Inn. He went on to become the Organist and Choirmaster in Bodmin and was offered the same position in Fowey Church in 1979.

Derek French married a local girl, Averil Sleep, in 1955

Jamaica Inn in the late 1940's, clearly showing the grass mound that used to cover the water tanks.

and he and his wife lived in Bolventor until 1995 when Derek moved away to Liskeard, after the sad loss of his wife. They were some of the linchpins - along with many others - who saw to it that the village community spirit lived on as long as it did. Before his retirement Derek also worked both at Hawks Tor and Park Clay Works. He tells the tale that three men were sent one day to check down the pipeline, to try and find a leak in the pipe which took the clay by natural gravity down to the Glyn Valley. The men became seperated, one going on one side, the other two together on the other side of the line. The man on his own lost sight of the others and turned back calling, "Have you found anything?" There was no answer so he retraced his steps until he came upon both men standing across the line. They stood motionless, staring, both mesmerised by what was described as a red adder, which was coiled a few feet away with its head raised and gently moving from side to side. Only when its head was cut off with the spade carried by the third man, did the men come out of their trance. These adders or vipers, both red and black, are peculiar to moorland, the red being female and the black unusually aggressive. Local folklore has it that they can leap at prey when provoked and will swallow their young to protect them if disturbed and then regurgitate them back.

The end of the war saw the end of Claude Finnamore's tenancy from Walter Dennis, who then began to sell off the individual land and properties, and the REAL changes in the old Coaching Inn as it had stood for nearly two hundred years, finally began.

Chapter seven

Fundamental Changes

Jamaica Inn's water supply was for a long time pumped by water-wheel from the stream that runs through the grounds of the old Vicarage. From there it was pumped into two large 500 gallon holding tanks in the loft of the Inn, and some of it was then drawn off outside into two very large slate tanks, hidden under a huge dry stone walled grassy mound in an oval shape, which started several feet from the Inn door and backed onto the road wall. The entrance and exit gateways were to the left and right of the mound which was placed there - with the tanks - sometime during the 19th Century, making a sweeping drive round for vehicles and coaches. On the road side of the wall, below where the Inn sign now hangs, there was a tap from which the villagers could draw their water supply the road then being some three feet lower than it is today.

The Inn looked much as it always had at that point. There were flower beds beneath the old sash windows and climbing roses round the porch. The mound, too, was covered with grass and shrubs and there was no low wall before the Inn. The coach house end of the stable block had a wall between it and the main road wall, and there was no side entrance to the Inn then. Round the mound were three magnificent slate and lead drinking troughs, and another one was in the courtyard. There was a walled garden to the right of the Inn. By using a local water diviner, in the mid fifties, the Council discovered water in one of the fields at the back of the Inn and a bore hole was sunk with the water being eventually pumped into a holding tank on the Dozmary Road. Reg Carthew was asked to check it daily for two weeks, to top it up with diesel and make sure that the water was flowing continually. At about this time a good part of the land at the back of the Jamaica Inn cottages was given to the Council in exchange for water rights to the bore hole and the three Council houses - now privately owned - were erected, a bank being built up between the new houses and old cottages where the cottagers' three peat stacks had formerly been.

In June 1945 when Stanley Thomas bought the Inn for £5,000, he applied for - and was granted - a license to turn it into a Club. It became known as the "Famous Jamaica Inn West Country Club". Membership was one shilling per year. Even though it had been a Temperance House before that it had always been possible to buy alcohol. Between 1946 and 1949 three applications were made for a full license to turn it into a Pub and were rejected. There was strong local opposition, particularly from the Methodist Minister and one of the local farmers, but it

The Inn Courtyard after the mound had been removed. The tap used by villagers to draw their water can be clearly seen under the new Inn sign.
Reproduced by kind permission of the Cornish Studies Library.

The Inn in the late forties, during its time as the West Country Club, showing the mound.

The Inn duriong the 1950's showing the Inn sign erected by Stanley Thomas.
Reproduced by kind permission of the Cornish Studies Library.

was interesting to note that when the full license was finally granted, the farmer's daughter was one of the first local people to apply for a job! When Stanley Thomas became the owner of Jamaica Inn, it was in a sorry state. The building was rotten with woodworm, it had dreadful old linoleum on the floors of most of the rooms, and both the Inn and the land around it were infested by rats. To Mr Thomas fell the task of trying to stop the rot and begin to restore the badly neglected building.

It was during Mr Thomas' ownership that the earth mound was demolished, the watertanks removed and more cobbles were brought from Plymouth bus routes - when the old trolley lines were taken up - to complete the cobbled courtyard, which became the first car park. Unfortunately the drinking troughs were just thrown out. It was then that the low wall in front of the Inn was built, and the old sash windows taken out to be replaced by shuttered, pseudo Victorian windows. In 1954 Mr Thomas also purchased the Jamaica Cottages and shortly after the 23 acres of land between the A30 and the St. Cleer road, together with the cottage which was the former Smithy. The Jamaica Cottages purchase was to enable Mr Thomas to use the buildings for overflow guests from the Inn but they were not interested in staying there and it became what is now known as the Staff Annexe. The last occupants there, the Janes family, were paid to move out so that the Annexe could be

renovated. Mr Thomas had to ask Reg Carthew to make a show of living there, as there was a housing shortage and he was afraid that it would be requisitioned. The Inn was very different in those days. Once through the porch door the stairs went straight up in front of you. To the right was the big open lounge which went through to what had been the original bar (where the Joss Merlyn figure is now). To the left of the door and stairs was the dining room. A passageway went right across the width of the Inn from west to east, and on the other side of the passage were the kitchens and the old store room. Following the passage west you came to the two ladies' toilets and on your left another doorway into the

The Inn during the fifties.

The Dining Room during the fifties.

The Lounge and Great Fireplace during the fifties.

Manager's office and the back stairs. There were no men's toilets then. Male customers would use the outside wall between the Inn and the calf shed, until there were strong objections voiced by local people who used that passageway for access to the moor. This forced the owners to build the first lavatories for men in part of the calf shed and - at varying times over the following years - these lavatories were extended more and more for both ladies and gents, gradually taking over all of that outbuilding. What had been the cow shed behind the stable block became the restaurant, and a passageway was knocked through from the Manager's office to connect up with the restaurant.

Where Potter's Museum stood, alongside the old calf shed, was the walled garden of the Inn, where fruit and vegetables were grown. In this garden - so local memory has it - sometime in the 19th Century there grew a tree - probably a Savin tree, member of the Juniper family - and an infusion made from the leaves of this tree was said to bring about a miscarriage when drunk. This brew was supposedly used to induce an abortion by Marie Hamilton, one of Mary, Queen of Scots' four famous Maries who were her ladies in waiting. Marie Hamilton had become pregnant by the King. The tree was used by local maidens around the moor and was eventually chopped down by an irate villager. The garden also fell victim to the boom in business after the full license was granted and was cleared, the wall knocked down and

The Lounge of Joss' Bar during the fifties.

levelled and the area was tarmacked to extend the car park.

In the process of knocking through another doorway, from the window end of the big lounge into what had been the Post Office - now the children's room - Reg Carthew discovered two more fireplaces. The existing one at that time was in the centre of the dividing wall, and copper canopied. A small one was found to the right when the doorway was knocked through and the old, original inglenook - now restored - was discovered when the dividing wall between it and the copper canopied fireplace fell down. The newly discovered Coat of Arms fireback in the inglenook, from the 19th Century, split one night in the mid fifties through frost coming down the chimney and had to be replaced - it is not known what happened to the original one - and the oak beam lintel of the inglenook unfortunately caught fire. Reg put the fire out with a soda syphon but the damage was extensive and he replaced the lintel with the granite one now there, from Carbilly Quarry.

The Post Office moved down to Deep Hatches, at the foot of the hill west of the Inn, and became the new centre for post-war purchase of dried milk, Cod Liver Oil and Orange Juice. The first 'shop' within the Inn was just two shelves near the bar, selling postcards and a few souvenirs, including some models of the Inn in Boscastle Pottery. A proper gift shop was then opened in the stable block where the coach house was and the Du Maurier room is today. With one brief change it stayed there until 1990, when it moved to its present site, using and renovating the building first put up as a garage by William Palmer. In 1994 it was again enlarged.

Mr Thomas did not live on the premises and had a quick succession of Managers until Mr and Mrs Grose came to work for him. Mr Grose had been in the Life Guards and was an ex-prisoner of war. The Groses were with Mr Thomas for almost ten years and helped with the transition from Country Club to Public House. Mrs Grose died at the Inn and her coffin was put out on the wall for the Undertakers to collect! During the Grose's stewardship around 1952, there was one of the worst

Fundamental Chages

The Inn on the Moor, A History of Jamaica Inn

The Inglenook fireplace with the original wooden lintel that caught fire in the 1950's.

The Inglenook fireplace with the granite lintel, put in by Reg Carthew.

Bolventor Harrier's Boxing Day Meet 1950.
Photograph loaned by Derek French.

winters ever experienced on the moors. In the hollow between the top of Palmer's Bridge Hill and Bolventor snow lay fifteen foot deep and was eventually cleared by hand by men with shovels, and lorries to take it away. Stock had to be fed and a helicopter was sent out to drop feed for the moor livestock, but it lost the top of its rotor blade and was marooned on Catshole for five days. The Mayor of Bodmin and his party, on their way home, were also forced to halt at the Inn seeking shelter and they too, were stuck at the Inn for several days.

The long disused Davidstow airfield became a Motor Racing circuit in 1949 for a few years and many of the drivers and teams who came to use the circuit also stayed at Jamaica Inn, including the Princes Chula and Bira of Siam. The Inn plays host for many occasions including wedding receptions and one such memorable occasion was the celebration in Joss' Bar of the marriage of Annie and Frank Harrison around 1967, during which occurred the usual trouble trying to get the fire to burn up. George Reddicliffe - another very well known local character - proceeded to cut up his wellies to feed to the fire, to make it burn!

In 1961 Stanley Thomas sold the 23 acres of land that he had bought to Mary Wonnacott, who moved into the Jamaica Inn Farmhouse and in November 1962 he sold Jamaica Inn to William Alfred and Margaret Laura Palmer, from Leicester, for £22,000. This sum included the annexe and the Jamaica Inn Farmhouse. The Palmers were the only owners of Jamaica Inn to live there with their family, and use it as a home.

CHAPTER EIGHT

Alistair Maclean

By the time that Mr and Mrs Palmer took over the ownership of Jamaica Inn, the fundamental changes carried out by their predecessor had - for the first time - really altered the outside appearance of the Inn. Many minor alterations had occurred inside it's walls, but the courtyard and surrounding garden and fields had remained much as they had always been. There is no doubt that those first alterations took away much of the character of the old Jamaica Inn.

More alterations were to take place during the two years that the Palmers were residing at the Inn. It was Mr Palmer who connected the Inn to the outside toilets (former calf shed), by putting a roof across to make a covered way for storing the beer barrels and it was a very controversial move which greatly upset the local villagers, who had been in the habit of using that pathway for their access to the moor. The dispute lasted for years and later owners were eventually involved in litigation over the rights of way and were subsequently fined. However, this did not seem to be very fair as the Deed plans showed the definite right of way as being to the west of the Inn, and round the building to the back. The long-running dispute became totally irrelevant anyway, when the village was by-passed in 1993 and the new dual carriageway came between the village and the moor.

During the building of the road, the old toll house down at Palmer's Bridge and the two cottages alongside it were mysteriously demolished overnight by the road builders and this, more than anything antagonised local people, since there was absolutely no need for the demolition. Another piece of their history was gone.

Mr Palmer built the garage which is now the Inn gift shop and he also moved the shop from the stable block back into the Inn. The dining room to the left of the front door became the shop.

One of the Inn's more colourful Managers was Peter Mositano, who was first employed in 1960 by Stanley Thomas. He it was who would, without any warning, approach his customers and cut off the ends of their ties! This motley collection of tie ends is still pinned up above the outer door of the children's room, and includes part of an upside down parachute tie, given to survivors of Para drops where the chute failed to open. The main beams in the bar are also covered with old bank notes from all over the world. That collection has been building up since the 1950's. Whilst Mositano was at the Inn, he supervised the opening of the Stable bar and he turned the back kitchen into the Pedlar's Bar (where the Pool room now is). The small closet that had been the first gent's lavatory - now just a part of the beer storeroom - he transformed into an ice cream parlour!

Peter Mositano and Mr Palmer however, did not really see eye to eye and Mr Mositano had left the Inn by the time that it was sold again, only two years later in 1964. On the 27th July, of that year, it passed into the hands of it's most famous owner, Alistair Maclean, (Maclean Nominees) for the sum of £27,500.

Alistair Maclean was the Gaelic speaking son of a strict Scottish Minister, and a Graduate with an MA from the Glasgow University. His father never really approved of him. Alistair served in the Royal Navy during the War, his ship being part of the grim, hazardous Murmansk Convoys and his experiences helped him begin to write, H.M.S. Ulysses being the first bestseller of many.

A diffident man about his own talent, he always seemed to give the impression that he was ashamed of the work he turned out, as if the books were somehow less worthy because they were thriller action fiction - maybe he thought his father would not think them worthwhile - and he never allowed his books to be sold at the Inn shop. Sylvia Kestell, of Higher St. Luke's Farm, worked for Alistair Maclean serving in the gift shop, which was then still in the former dining room of the Inn. She remembers how they would normally stock his books which sold very well, but when they knew that he would be coming to the Inn they would hastily remove the books and hide them until he had gone. Both she and Reg Carthew remember him as a 'real gentleman'.

The village War Memorial Cross had stood for many years on the corner of the Dozmary road, just in front of the Jamaica Cottages and the Council, wishing to widen the road at that point, paid £200 to Mr Maclean to allow them to re-site the Cross on a piece of land belonging to the Inn, just opposite it where it still is today. He also applied for and was granted a £2,759 Grant in 1972, to redevelop the Inn as a Hotel and part of that money was used to convert more of the stable block, creating a Manager's flat above it.

Mr Maclean was very much an absentee owner, having many other commitments. He only actually stayed once at the Inn for a period of three days, in May 1972, flying in and out of Treswithick Airfield by private plane. His brother, Captain Maclean, helped to oversee the running of the Inn, doing the interviewing of staff and so on. There were a succession of Managers in the eleven years that Alistair Maclean owned Jamaica Inn and it never prospered enough to realise the investment he thought he had made in buying the Inn to leave to his children. As a result, in 1973, the Inn was again put on the market. Mr and Mrs Palmer did try to buy it back, but it was eventually sold to its present owners, John and Wendy Watts, on 3rd December 1973, for the sum of £57,500, plus a further £6,000 for fixtures and fittings. In passing into the hands of Mr and Mrs Watts, under whose ownership it has become a flourishing concern, the Inn was to finally pull away from its past and move towards the next Century, confidently going forward to welcome many thousands more visitors through its portals.

The original site of the village War Memorial Cross, Young David Sleep and Billy Winn in foreground.
Reproduced by kind permission of the Cornish Studies Library.

CHAPTER NINE

Significant Changes

In the ensuing years to date, since the Jamaica Inn's last change of ownership, there have been many significant changes, not only in the Inn but in the life of Bolventor too.

The Inn itself has had radical alterations both inside and out, though the front view of the Inn and stableblock has changed little and looks much as it always has done since the post-war tentative changes - from a facade point of view. The first known Inn sign, erected in the fifties by Stanley Thomas and which swung outside the Inn for nearly forty years, was replaced in the early nineties. The original one can be seen at the Inn gift shop. The shop was moved back out into the stable block until 1990, when it was moved into the new premises, the specially reconstructed garage to the western rear of the Inn. This shop has again doubled in size since then.

Dame Daphne Du Maurier, who was created a Dame of the British Empire in 1969, died in 1989. A very private woman all her life who shunned much of the publicity she could have enjoyed, her funeral was a simple affair, involving only the immediate family and a few very close friends. She was cremated and her ashes were scattered on the Menabilly Estate that she loved so much. A quiet thanksgiving service in her memory was held in the small Tregaminion Church on the Estate. In recognition of her contribution to Cornish life and her achievments in the literary world, a Dame Daphne Du Maurier memorial Room was set up where the shop had been in the stable block. Mr and Mrs Watts were able to purchase one of her writing desks and other personal mementos at the sale of her belongings and other pieces were generously donated by the Browning family. The room was opened by her grandson, Robert Browning, on 11th April 1990. This memorial room was incorporated into the new Smuggler's Museum, when it was transferred from its original site in the old village school, to the stable block and old cow shed (former restaurant), at the Inn.

Inside the Inn the wall to the left was demolished and moved back further, to leave a much smaller area which is now the reception and office. The main stair-case was also moved over to the reception area. This meant that the inglenook lounge became much bigger and the main bar was built into that room, on the left-hand wall. The passageway, running from east to west of the Inn, was also partly removed thus creating the Pool room and, later on, the first specially designated Snack Bar was added to the back of the Inn, a large extension which is now called the Pedlar's Bar and that, too, has more than doubled in size in the last few years. A new toilet block was built between shop and snack bar, to high standards. Upstairs

The old Inn sign which was replaced in the early 1990's.

The Restaurant in the Old Stable Block before the room became part of the Smuggler's Museum in 2003.
Reproduced by kind permission of the Cornish Studies Library.

Percy with Graham Watts.

the accommodation was also updated and the Inn now has six en-suite bedrooms to house guests. Additional bedrooms are planned for the near future.

Mr and Mrs Watts, though not resident at the Inn, are frequently there and their interest in the business, and the staff, remains constant. The last of the long serving Managers to Mr and Mrs Watts were Eddie and Rose Lee and Jim and Dot Manson, who have moved on to pastures new. The longest resident of all, of course, is Percy! Percy is also, by far and away, the champion character. Bought to the Inn by Reg Carthew nearly forty years ago, his exact age is unknown. Thought for years, until the early nineties, to be a cock mackaw, he (she!) began laying eggs at a rate of knots in 1991, leaving everyone with egg on their faces! Having been called Percy for so many years there seemed little point in trying to rename her. She is cantankerous and loving - depending on her mood - her language is ripe. Having persistently plucked most of her chest feathers out for years, though healthy, loved and cared for, she looked a mess and it was decided in the year 2000 to retire her, away from her public appearances.

Because of the isolation of Bolventor and the increasing number of visitors who come to the Inn each year, Mr and Mrs Watts began looking round for some other attraction to bring to Bolventor for their visitors to enjoy and they found that very thing when Potter's Museum of Curiosity was put up for sale in West Sussex. This unique Museum was founded by Victorian Taxidermist, Walter Potter, in 1861 in Bramber, West Sussex. Though frowned upon by some people today, taxidermy (whose original purpose was educational, in exhibiting unknown species) was a very popular hobby and trade in Victorian times. It was both normal and acceptable and Walter Potter was simply a man of those times.

Begun as a hobby in his teens and starting with the preservation of his pet canary when it died, the taxidermy work took over his life after the creation of his first large tableau, "The Death and Burial of Cock Robin". The idea for the tableau came to him after seeing an illustrated copy of the poem in his small sister's book and was the solution to the problem of what to do with his ever growing collection of stuffed birds. The tableau took him nearly seven years to complete in his spare time. It attracted a lot of interest when first put on display in his garden shed and people began to start paying a few coppers to come and see this marvel. Potter's father once owned the local Inn, The White Lion (later renamed The Castle Hotel), and when he sold it to a Brewery, the Brewery, seeing the potential revenue to be gained by encouranging people to come and see Walter's growing collection, built a house for him and his family and the Museum really began to do well. The Museum stayed in the Potter family for over a hundred years until the early

"The Kitten's Wedding" - Tableau by Walter Potter on exhibit in the Potter's Museum of Curiosity.

"The Guinea Pig's Cricket Match" - Tableau by Walter Potter on exhibit in the Potter's Museum of Curiosity.

1970's, when it moved briefly to Brighton and from there to Arundel, where it stayed until bought by Mr and Mrs Watts in the late 1980's.

The whole Museum was packed up and moved down to Cornwall to the Inn and a building adjoining the outside lavatories (the old calf shed) was erected to house the Museum. In keeping with the shop, the snack bars and other alterations, the plan of the new building was sympathetically designed to blend into the old Inn. The Museum was opened by Lady Lucinda Lambton on 20th May 1988.

As well as the unique collection of Walter Potter's tableaux, including the Kitten's Wedding, The Victorian Rabbit School and many others, the Museum has been greatly added to by its present owners who are very keen collectors, and finally comprised some 10,000 artifacts and curiosities from all over the world, including the Turf Iron used by Sam Sleep, Averil French's Father. The collection built up a well deserved reputation for being one of the most interesting little Museums in the country. One extension has been added to it already and no doubt there will be others! Mr and Mrs Watts also acquired a collection of Smuggling Artifacts and a completely new "Experience" opened in the old school house (which is just across the road from the Inn, a little way down the St. Cleer Road), in 1998.

This attraction in three parts, designed to appeal to the whole family, uses the latest digital technology but with traditional methods of interpretation.

It begins with an introduction to the life and works of Dame Daphne Du Maurier, and goes onto a theatrical presentation of the story of the book "Jamaica Inn", told in tableaux, light and sound and ends with probably one of the finest collections of smuggling relics from the ancient to the modern, as smuggling alas is not something relating only to the dim and distant past. The project has been designed and built by Concepts and Interpretations, and a great deal of valued assistance has been given by Kits Browning, Daphne Du Maurier's son. The voice of Cornwall narrates the story, and the gentleman with the authentic Cornish voice was chosen after a competition was held to judge the most suitable narrator for this exciting new attraction. The Smuggler's Museum was transferred to the Inn complex in 2003, and the Potter's Museum was closed, and sold, that same year.

The decision to close Potter's was reluctantly taken by Mr and Mrs Watts. They had retired and were no longer able to work on the Museum and I was due to retire. But the biggest blow of all, resulting in the final decision of closure, was the sudden illness, and untimely death, of Michael Ryan Grace in 2002.

Michael was the skilled taxidermist and maintenance man, who had taken care of the collection for many years, and the owners felt that he would be irreplaceable.

Over the years the Inn has played host to many famous faces, among them Jack Higgins (author of the Eagle has Landed), who was a friend of Alistair Maclean's, Patricia Phoenix (Elsie Tanner), who had a home in Zennor, down near Land's End, some of the Crossroads Cast, and also members of the Black and White Minstrels, to name but a few. Most of the sponsored Charity Walkers have also dropped in or stayed, including Dr. Barbara Moore, Ian Botham, Jethro (the Cornish Comedian), who was raising money for an open scanner and one of the West Country's best known Charity Walkers, Det. Sgt. Eric Wallis. In 1980 on one of his 250 mile sponsored walks he had to take shelter in Jamaica Inn after heavy snow made him turn back from attempting to climb Brown Willy.

Sadly, where the Inn has gone from strength to strength, Bolventor is no longer the close-knit community that it was in the old days. Although the Church was re-hallowed in August of 1965, its Congregation declined steadily to the point where on the 10th June 1981, "By Order of Her Majesty in Council, The Holy Trinity Church (excluding the Church Yard), was taken out of the Parochial System under a declaration of Redundancy." The Church is gradually decaying in the moorland wind and weather.

The Methodist Chapel of St. Luke's is still regularly attended, but only now by some dozen or so hardy souls including Marian Bunney, who was the Organist at the Chapel for many years and who talked to us at length and so kindly loaned us her entire collection of scrapbooks, put together by her father, her husband and herself over a fifty year period and from which we obtained so much useful and interesting information. Gone are the Dozmary Picnic days, the Sportsdays, the Gymkhanas and the Horticultural Shows. Now, instead of a pleasant moorland vista, the upper St. Neot Valley has become Colliford Lake. Begun in 1979 and flooded in 1981 it now contains some 6,395 million gallons of water (2,900 megalitres). Excavation done prior to the commencement revealed a tin mine, dating from 1500, many Stone Age flint artifacts, a Bronze Age burial mound and a large medieval farming settlement - all gone to the deep! Most of the shoreline is deep mud and very dangerous and the lake is not suitable for the watersports seen on so many reservoirs as the valley trees were not cut down and removed.

The Sub Post Office at Deep Hatches was compulsorily bought by South West Water in 1977 for the Reservoir Scheme and though not ultimately affected by the construction of the lake, was never re-opened though permission was sought. In the same way the loss of the old Toll House was a considerable blow. It can never be put back.

Many of the moorland farms fell into disuse, but some of these have - at least - been purchased and restored, converted into lovely homes, bringing much needed life again to the moor. The Bolventor School, from 100 pupils when it opened in 1879 was down to just one by 1990 and it closed in 1991. Another sad day for the people of Bolventor, though the schoolhouse, too, was saved by Mr and Mrs Watts and was privately sold in 2003 after the Smuggler's Museum was transferred to the Inn.

Sylvia Kestell and her aunt Vera are now the only real Bolventorians left, though the 'immigrant' population, like myself, care as much for our adopted homeland as do the people who were born in Cornwall, for it is indeed something very special, there is nowhere like it - a land apart.

Still, there are SOME things that do not change. The high moors do not change. The sunrises and sunsets are still wondrous to behold, the gorse, blackthorn, whitethorn and briar still bloom, the sloes, blackberries and whortleberries are still harvested every year and the tors, trees and chimneys still rise up out of the season's mists. In the harsh winter of 1996/7, the craggy faces of the quarries were still bedecked with giant icicles that reached in layers from the top to the frozen ground beneath, resembling a great, magnificent, glittering Cathedral Organ, as they are so bedecked in every such spell of cold weather. Still easy then to imagine the Coach Drivers with their heavy great-coats and sturdy postilion boots, cracking the whip, blowing the horn, urging on their teams of sweating, straining horses to climb that last hill, to find the warmth and shelter at the top that is the Jamaica Inn.

Today in Cornwall there is but one working tin mine left, South Crofty, and even that constantly hovers on the brink of closure. The once great fishing industry of Cornwall has been decimated and both farming and the China Clay industry face ever increasing pressures. The lifeblood of this great county is tourism, and tourism is its main hope for the future. To all readers who still lament the passing of the old days and the changes to the old Coaching Inn that they once knew, I say, "Be grateful for the changes and for the caring owners who have produced the Jamaica Inn of today for it - like any other business - MUST adapt, or die."

THE END

Special Thanks and Acknowledgements

Marian Bunney

Sylvia Kestell

Phyllis Best

Mr and Mrs T. Johns

Reg Carthew

Derek French

George Reddicliffe

Harry Patterson

David Smith

Paul Tyler, MP

The Foreign and Commonwealth Officer

The Royal Horticultural Society

Michael Latham

County Records Office - Truro

The Cornish Studies Library - Redruth

and The Public Library - Launceston